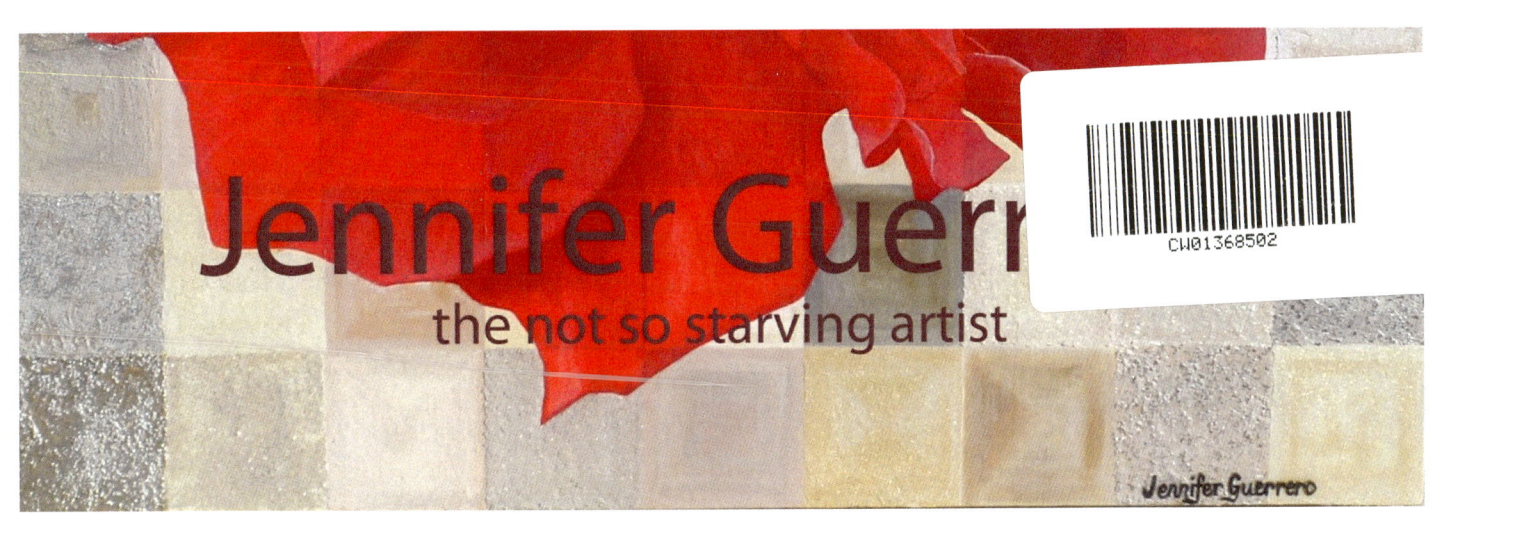

Jen's Protein Nice Creams 2,
Unofficial guide to high-protein ice creams in the Ninja Creami™ Deluxe
Copyright © 2024 by Jennifer Guerrero
www.JenniferGuerrero.com

Photo Credits: All photography in this book was taken by Jennifer Guerrero.

All rights reserved. No part of this publication may be reproduced, distributed, or transmitted in any form or by any means, including photocopying, recording, or other electronic or mechanical methods, without the prior written permission of the author, except in the case of brief quotations embodied in critical reviews and certain other non-commercial uses permitted by copyright law.

Jen's Protein Nice Creams 2

Nutrition facts for 12 oz (1/2 container)	Protein (g)	Fat (g)	Carbs (g)	Calories	Page
Carrot Cake	39	7	33	288	10
Cantaloupe	38	4	29	263	11
Blueberry Lemonade	37	4	47	266	12
Apricot Sundae	39	4	65	433	13
Red Raspberry	41	5	26	294	14
Raspberry Hibiscus kisses	38	5	28	233	15
Strawberry Rhubarb	37	4	42	249	16
Blackberry	40	5	47	310	17
Mango Daiquiri (NO ALCOHOL)	39	5	51	341	18
Cherry Limeade	38	4	46	311	19
Sour Apple Candy	37	4	36	303	20
Hummingbird Cake	39	18	58	438	21
Dragonfruit	38	5	37	278	22
Passionfruit	38	5	58	270	23
Coconut	38	12	21	308	24
Candied Orange Sweet Potato	42	12	49	406	25
Strawberry Special K	41	5	41	314	26
Special K	50	8	39	363	27
Mint Chocolate Chip	38	14	52	369	28
Lavender Honey	38	5	61	417	29
Chai	41	9	32	359	30
Coffee	37	4	33	216	31
Matcha	38	6	38	246	32
Butter Pecan	40	20	28	369	33
Salted Caramel Pretzel	41	5	21	273	34
Gingerbread	38	5	60	308	35
Chocolate Hazelnut	42	24	42	458	36
Chocolate Dipped Churro	38	7	39	280	37
Loaded Chile Chocolate	46	21	50	469	38
Kinda Feel Like an Almond Joy	39	13	40	345	39
BONUS Jen's Protein Brandy Slush	37	4	57	369	40-41

Thank you so much for picking up a copy of my 2nd book! I've given all my attention to creating protein-filled ice cream that tastes decadent and delicious. Boom. The flavors and textures are perfect. These would make any foodie smile. I am obsessed! I'm super excited to share them with all of you! Hope you love them, too!

xx Jen

Okay! You've memorized the instruction manual and you're ready to go!

Things that might help....

Texture: All the creamis in this book are cottage cheese and protein powder based. "Light ice cream" will give you something between soft serve and a smoothie bowl. It requires less re-spins. An insulated cup will help it from melting quickly. I use this setting whenever I want soft serve in an insulated cup. "Ice cream" gives a firmer texture. I use this whenever I want a bowl of firm scoopable ice cream.

ICE CREAM	LITE ICE CREAM
Designed for traditionally indulgent recipes. Great for turning dairy and dairy-alternative recipes into thick, creamy, and scoopable ice creams.	Designed for health-conscious consumers to make ice creams that are low in sugar or fat or use sugar substitutes. Choose when processing keto, paleo, or vegan recipes.

Salt: Adding a pinch of salt to desserts to enhance flavor is all the rage. No need to do that here! Cottage cheese is a little salty, and will take case of that enhancement for you.

Flavor: I am a massive flavorist. I made notes on some of the recipes about how important—or not—the mix-ins are to the flavor so that you can make the right decision for you!

Size: All of my recipes fill a 24 ounce Deluxe Creami container. If you have a Ninja Creami with 16 ounce containers, you'll just do 2/3 of each recipe. OR double the recipe and fill (3) 16-ounce containers.

Must have...

A Ninja Creami ice cream maker. Everything in this book is made for the Ninja Creami Deluxe, the 24 oz size. If you have a smaller 16 oz Ninja Creami, you'll have to scale the recipes to 2/3.

Nice to have...

An immersion (stick) blender. This is a lazy human's dream. Just insert it right into your Creami container and blend away. Yes, you could totally do this with a food processor, but this is much more streamlined and easier to clean up. I wouldn't recommend a hand mixer and bowl. It has a terrible time blending up the cottage cheese nicely.

Wine glass covers. When you put your blended base into the freezer for 24 hours, and pull it out, lots of times there's a weird frozen hump coming out of it like a little alien. What happened? Things expand when they freeze. We don't want that weird frozen growth to break our blade! What to do? Some people take a knife and shave it down. Others swear by leaving the container cover off til it's fully frozen. I like to pop a wine glass cover right on top of the mixture and then add the cover.

Everyone has personal preferences about ingredients. I have very intentionally included the protein, fat, carbs, and calories by ingredient so that you can easily swap in for your own preferences.

Ingredients I'm using....

Cottage cheese—Daisy 2%

Protein Powders
Optimum Nutrition vanilla ice cream
Optimum Nutrition extreme milk chocolate
Ryse Jet-Puffed
Quest Salted Caramel

Swerve
Regular
Brown Sugar
Confectioners

Extracts
Vanilla
Almond
Rum
Butter
Strawberry
Mango
Coconut
Mint
Buttery Sweet Dough
Cream cheese icing
Pecan

Boatloads of frozen fruit, nuts, unsweetened cocoa powder, mini chocolate chips, coconut, some cookies and candies, a sugar free Jell-o.....

Substitutions

<u>Milk</u> Can you use a different milk than almond milk? Absolutely!!! I love the flavor of almond milk, but definitely use your family's favorite milk!

<u>Cottage Cheese</u> Can you sub in anything for cottage cheese? Yes! Tofu! Tofu ranges from silky to firm. The silky has a milder flavor and less protein. The flavor is more pronounced in extra firm, but it has much higher protein counts....

I subbed in **half a block of well-drained firm tofu** for cottage cheese. I tried it on blueberry and strawberry. You could detect it in the blueberry, but it wasn't screaming for attention. It worked perfectly in the strawberry! None of us would have a preference between the cottage cheese and to-fruity strawberry! They did require extra sweetener, though - 1 extra Tablespoon in the blueberry and 2 in the strawberry, and a little extra almond milk in the re-spin. I tested fruit because the chocolate would definitely cover it.

LITE ICE CREAM

Designed for health-conscious consumers to make ice creams that are low in sugar or fat or use sugar substitutes. Choose when processing keto, paleo, or vegan recipes.

Tofu Cottage Cheese difference				
Daisy 2% cottage cheese 1 cup	26	5	10	180
Firm Tofu 8 oz	19	11	5	187
Tofu difference (whole 24 ounce container)	-7	6	-5	7
For half of a container...	Protein	Fat	Carbs	Calories
Wild Blueberry	37	4	32	280
Wild Blueberry - tofu	33	7	29	283
For half of a container...	Protein	Fat	Carbs	Calories
Strawberry	37	4	26	250
Strawberry - tofu	33	7	23	253

Overall.... For half of a container...

Tofu 4 grams **protein** less

Tofu 3 grams **fat** more

Tofu 3 grams **carbs** less

Tofu 3 **calories** more

If you are new to tofu, cut it into cubes, wrap it in a bunch of paper towel, put a heavy pot on it, and let it drain for 15 minutes. Ready to use!

You blended it! If it looks super creamy, you're ready. It looks crumbly? That is totally normal. Add 1-2 Tablespoons of Almond milk and hit "full" "re-spin".

You can skip the extra almond milk and just hit re-spin if it's close...

Less almond milk = firmer ice cream

More almond milk = soft-servier ice cream.

Re-spin?

Ready for mix-ins? Awesome! Sometimes the machine leaves a well right up the center of the creami. If not, make one! Make your column as evenly as you can from the very bottom to the top so the goodies will get distributed evenly. Chop up those goodies!

They don't all fit???? Overflow are just toppings!

Press "full" and mix-ins".

Mix-ins

Anatomy of a Mix-In

Does the order you add the mix-ins in matter? Totally! When you press that mix-in button, the blade spins and distributes the mix-ins at the same height they're at in the container.

If you drop chopped up frozen raspberries in the bottom half and mini chocolate chips in the top, the bottom half will be filled with little raspberry chunks and the top will be polka-dotted with chocolate chips. Cool if two people strongly disagree about what the mix-in should be.

If you mix up your mix-ins before you drop them in, the whole container will get little pops of raspberries and chocolate. Basically nirvana.

Carrot Cake

Ingredient	Protein	Fat	Carbs	Calories
1 cup 2% Daisy cottage cheese	26	5	10	180
2 scoops vanilla protein powder (Optimum Nutrition Whey)	48	3	8	240
1 1/2 cups carrot juice (Bolthouse Farms is lovely)	3	0	23	105
1/2 teaspoon ground cinnamon				
1/8 teaspoon ground ginger				
pinch of ground cloves				
2 Tablespoons walnuts	1	5	1	50
1/4 teaspoon lorann super strength cream cheese icing flavor				
1 teaspoon vanilla extract				
2 Tablespoons brown sugar Swerve	0	0	24	0
Total	78	13	66	575
Half of that big old 24 oz Deluxe container	39	7	33	288

1. Measure all the base ingredients into your Creami container, making sure not to pass the max fill line.
2. Blend with your immersion (stick) blender til smooth and luscious.
3. Pop into your freezer for 24 hours.
4. Pop into your Ninja Creami Deluxe. Select full, make your selection, and hit the go button.
5. Take a peek. Perfectly creamy? Great! If not, add 1-2 Tablespoons of vanilla almond milk and select full and push the re-spin button. (Usually requires a re-spin.
6. Enjoy!

Makes a 24 oz Deluxe pint. Have a smaller 16 oz model? Cut all the ingredients to 2/3.

Cantaloupe

	Protein	Fat	Carbs	Calories
1 cup 2% Daisy cottage cheese	26	5	10	180
2 scoops vanilla protein powder (Optimum Nutrition Whey)	48	3	8	240
2 cups cantaloupe, fresh and fragrant	3	1	27	106
1 Tablespoon Swerve	0	0	12	0
Total	77	9	57	526
Half of that big old 24 oz Deluxe container	**38**	**4**	**29**	**263**

My youngest drove up from her college and wanted an ice cream. She's a cookies and cream or chocolate peanut butter girl. There were two ice creams left in the freezer. No chocolate. She was not enthused. I handed her the cantaloupe and she tasted it. Her eyes got huge and she burst out, "Mama! This is the best one!" and walked off with the container and a spoon. Total mom victory!

1. Measure all the base ingredients into your Creami container, making sure not to pass the max fill line.
2. Blend with your immersion (stick) blender til smooth and luscious.
3. Pop into your freezer for 24 hours.
4. Pop into your Ninja Creami Deluxe. Select full, make your selection, and hit the go button.
5. Take a peek. Perfectly creamy? Great! If not, add 1-2 Tablespoons of vanilla almond milk and select full and push the re-spin button. (Usually requires a re-spin.
6. Enjoy!

Makes a 24 oz Deluxe pint. Have a smaller 16 oz model? Cut all the ingredients to 2/3.

Blueberry Lemonade

	Protein	Fat	Carbs	Calories
1 cup 2% Daisy cottage cheese	26	5	10	180
2 scoops vanilla protein powder (Optimum Nutrition Whey)	48	3	8	240
1 1/4 cups frozen blueberries, thawed (Wyman's wild)	0	0	24	100
1/4 cup fresh squeezed lemon juice	0	0	3	10
zest of 1/2 lemon	0	0	1	2
1/4 cup Swerve	0	0	48	0
Total	74	8	94	532
Half of that big old 24 oz Deluxe container	37	4	47	266

1. Measure all the base ingredients into your Creami container, making sure not to pass the max fill line.
2. Blend with your immersion (stick) blender til smooth and luscious.
3. Pop into your freezer for 24 hours.
4. Pop into your Ninja Creami Deluxe. Select full, make your selection, and hit the go button.
5. Take a peek. Perfectly creamy? Great! If not, add 1-2 Tablespoons of vanilla almond milk and select full and push the re-spin button. (Usually requires a re-spin.
6. Enjoy!

Measure frozen fruit while it's frozen!!!

Makes a 24 oz Deluxe pint. Have a smaller 16 oz model? Cut all the ingredients to 2/3.

Apricot Sundae

	Protein	Fat	Carbs	Calories
1 cup 2% Daisy cottage cheese	26	5	10	180
2 scoops vanilla protein powder (Optimum Nutrition Whey)	48	3	8	240
Apricot halves in light syrup, Del Monte 15 oz can	4	0	60	245
1 teaspoon vanilla extract				
Total	78	8	78	665
Half of that big old 24 oz Deluxe container	39	4	39	333
Drizzle! 2 Tablespoons Bonne Maman apricot preserves per person	0	0	26	100
Half plus apricot drizzle	39	4	65	433

1. Measure all the base ingredients into your Creami container, making sure not to pass the max fill line.
2. Blend with your immersion (stick) blender til smooth and luscious.
3. Pop into your freezer for 24 hours.
4. Pop into your Ninja Creami Deluxe. Select full, make your selection, and hit the go button.
5. Take a peek. Perfectly creamy? Great! If not, add 1-2 Tablespoons of vanilla almond milk and select full and push the re-spin button. (Usually requires a re-spin.
6. Enjoy!

Microwave the preserves for 20 seconds to make them runny for your topping!

Makes a 24 oz Deluxe pint. Have a smaller 16 oz model? Cut all the ingredients to 2/3.

Red Raspberry

Ingredient	Protein	Fat	Carbs	Calories
1 cup 2% Daisy cottage cheese	26	5	10	180
2 scoops vanilla protein powder (Optimum Nutrition Whey)	48	3	8	240
2 cups frozen red raspberries, thawed	4	2	34	120
1/4 cup vanilla almond milk	0	1	0	8
1 Tablespoon sugar free raspberry jell-o powder	4	0	0	40
Total	82	11	52	588
Half of that big old 24 oz Deluxe container	41	5	26	294

Don't want jell-o? Use 1 teaspoon raspberry extract and 1 Tablespoon swerve instead.

1. Measure all the base ingredients (not mix-ins or toppings!) into your Creami container, making sure not to pass the max fill line.
2. Blend with your immersion (stick) blender til smooth and luscious.
3. Pop into your freezer for 24 hours.
4. Pop into your Ninja Creami Deluxe. Select full, make your selection, and hit the go button.
5. Take a peek. Perfectly creamy? Great! If not, add 1-2 Tablespoons of vanilla almond milk and select full and push the re-spin button. (Usually requires a re-spin.
6. Enjoy!

Measure frozen fruit while it's frozen!!!

More frozen raspberries make a darling mix-in!

Makes a 24 oz Deluxe pint. Have a smaller 16 oz model? Cut all the ingredients to 2/3.

Raspberry Hibiscus Kisses

Ingredient	Protein	Fat	Carbs	Calories
1 cup 2% Daisy cottage cheese	26	5	10	180
2 scoops vanilla protein powder (Optimum Nutrition Whey)	48	3	8	240
1 1/2 cups concentrated hibiscus tea (*recipe below* ↓)	0	0	0	0
3/4 cup frozen raspberries, thawed	2	1	13	45
2 Tablespoons Swerve	0	0	24	0
1 teaspoon vanilla extract				
Total	76	9	55	465
Half of that big old 24 oz Deluxe container	38	5	28	233

Concentrated hibiscus tea
1 1/2 cups water
3/4 oz dried hibiscus flowers (Little less than 1/3 cup) (Frontier organic brand)
Pour boiling water over dried hibiscus flowers and let steep one hour. Strain. You're ready.

1. Measure all the base ingredients into your Creami container, making sure not to pass the max fill line.
2. Blend with your immersion (stick) blender til smooth and luscious.
3. Pop into your freezer for 24 hours.
4. Pop into your Ninja Creami Deluxe. Select full, make your selection, and hit the go button.
5. Take a peek. Perfectly creamy? Great! If not, add 1-2 Tablespoons of vanilla almond milk and select full and push the re-spin button. (Usually requires a re-spin.
6. Enjoy!

Measure frozen fruit while it's frozen!!!

Makes a 24 oz Deluxe pint. Have a smaller 16 oz model? Cut all the ingredients to 2/3.

Strawberry Rhubarb

	Protein	Fat	Carbs	Calories
1 cup 2% Daisy cottage cheese	26	5	10	180
2 scoops vanilla protein powder (Optimum Nutrition Whey)	48	3	8	240
3/4 cup frozen strawberries, thawed	0	0	9	34
1 1/4 cups frozen rhubarb, thawed	0	0	9	44
1/4 c brown sugar Swerve	0	0	48	0
1 teaspoon strawberry extract				
Total	74	8	84	498
Half of that big old 24 oz Deluxe container	37	4	42	249

Measure frozen fruit while it's frozen!!!

1. Measure all the base ingredients into your Creami container, making sure not to pass the max fill line.
2. Blend with your immersion (stick) blender til smooth and luscious.
3. Pop into your freezer for 24 hours.
4. Pop into your Ninja Creami Deluxe. Select full, make your selection, and hit the go button.
5. Take a peek. Perfectly creamy? Great! If not, add 1-2 Tablespoons of vanilla almond milk and select full and push the re-spin button. (Usually requires a re-spin.
6. Enjoy!

Lucky enough to have rhubarb growing in your yard? By all means, use fresh rhubarb! Freeze a few 1 1/4 cup bags to use when out of season!

Makes a 24 oz Deluxe pint. Have a smaller 16 oz model? Cut all the ingredients to 2/3.

Blackberry

	Protein	Fat	Carbs	Calories
1 cup 2% Daisy cottage cheese	26	5	10	180
2 scoops vanilla protein powder (Optimum Nutrition Whey)	48	3	8	240
2 1/2 cups frozen blackberry, thawed	5	1	53	200
2 Tablespoons Swerve	0	0	24	0
Total	79	9	95	620
Half of that big old 24 oz Deluxe container	40	5	47	310

Blackberries have a gentle berry flavor, so I 10/10 recommend adding more frozen blackberries as a mix-in. Bonus that it gives it little colorful flecks of cuteness.

1. Measure all the base ingredients (not mix-ins or toppings!) into your Creami container, making sure not to pass the max fill line.
2. Blend with your immersion (stick) blender til smooth and luscious.
3. Pop into your freezer for 24 hours.
4. Pop into your Ninja Creami Deluxe. Select full, make your selection, and hit the go button.
5. Take a peek. Perfectly creamy? Great! If not, add 1-2 Tablespoons of vanilla almond milk and select full and push the re-spin button. (Usually requires a re-spin.
6. Add in the **chopped up mix-ins** in a column up the center of the container and hit full, mix in.
7. Enjoy!

Measure frozen fruit while it's frozen!!!

Makes a 24 oz Deluxe pint. Have a smaller 16 oz model? Cut all the ingredients to 2/3.

Mango Daiquiri

Ingredient	Protein	Fat	Carbs	Calories
1 cup 2% Daisy cottage cheese	26	5	10	180
2 scoops vanilla protein powder (Optimum Nutrition Whey)	48	3	8	240
2 cups frozen mango, thawed	3	1	53	240
zest of 1/2 a lime	0	0	0	1
juice of 2 limes	0	0	7	20
2 Tablespoons Swerve	0	0	24	0
1 teaspoon mango extract				
1 teaspoon rum extract				
Optional: a few drops of yellow and red food coloring				
Total	77	9	102	681
Half of that big old 24 oz Deluxe container	**39**	**5**	**51**	**341**

1. Measure all the base ingredients into your Creami container, making sure not to pass the max fill line.
2. Blend with your immersion (stick) blender til smooth and luscious.
3. Pop into your freezer for 24 hours.
4. Pop into your Ninja Creami Deluxe. Select full, make your selection, and hit the go button.
5. Take a peek. Perfectly creamy? Great! If not, add 1-2 Tablespoons of vanilla almond milk and select full and push the re-spin button. (Usually requires a re-spin.
6. Enjoy!

Makes a 24 oz Deluxe pint. Have a smaller 16 oz model? Cut all the ingredients to 2/3.

Cherry Limeade

	Protein	Fat	Carbs	Calories
1 cup 2% Daisy cottage cheese	26	5	10	180
2 scoops vanilla protein powder (Optimum Nutrition Whey)	48	3	8	240
2 cups frozen cherries, thawed	2	0	44	180
2 Tablespoons Swerve	0	0	24	0
lime zest 1/2 lime	0	0	0	1
juice of 2 limes	0	0	7	20
total	76	8	93	621
Half of that big old 24 oz Deluxe container	**38**	**4**	**46**	**311**

1. Measure all the base ingredients (not mix-ins or toppings!) into your Creami container, making sure not to pass the max fill line.
2. Blend with your immersion (stick) blender til smooth and luscious.
3. Pop into your freezer for Pop into your Ninja Creami Deluxe. Select full, make your selection, and hit the go button.
4. Take a peek. Perfectly creamy? Great! If not, add 1-2 Tablespoons of vanilla almond milk and select full and push the re-spin button. (Usually requires a re-spin.
5. Enjoy!

Measure frozen fruit while it's frozen!!!

I added more frozen chopped up cherries as a mix-in. This totally looks like Valentine's or Galentine's Day!

Makes a 24 oz Deluxe pint. Have a smaller 16 oz model? Cut all the ingredients to 2/3.

Sour Apple Candy

Ingredient	Protein	Fat	Carbs	Calories
1 cup 2% Daisy cottage cheese	26	5	10	180
2 scoops vanilla protein powder (Optimum Nutrition Whey)	48	3	8	240
1 3/4 cups unsweetened apple sauce (Motts)	0	0	49	175
2 sugar free Jolly Rancher green apple drink mix packets	0	0	4	10
Total	74	8	71	605
Half of that big old 24 oz Deluxe container	**37**	**4**	**36**	**303**

1. Measure all the base ingredients into your Creami container, making sure not to pass the max fill line.
2. Blend with your immersion (stick) blender til smooth and luscious.
3. Pop into your freezer for 24 hours.
4. Pop into your Ninja Creami Deluxe. Select full, make your selection, and hit the go button.
5. Take a peek. Perfectly creamy? Great! If not, add 1-2 Tablespoons of vanilla almond milk and select full and push the re-spin button. (Usually requires a re-spin.
6. Enjoy!

Makes a 24 oz Deluxe pint. Have a smaller 16 oz model? Cut all the ingredients to 2/3.

Hummingbird Cake

Ingredient	Protein	Fat	Carbs	Calories
1 cup 2% Daisy cottage cheese	26	5	10	180
2 scoops vanilla protein powder (Optimum Nutrition Whey)	48	3	8	240
1 banana	1	0	27	105
1/2 cup crushed pineapple	0	0	17	70
1/4 cup unsweetened coconut flakes	2	14	5	140
1/4 cup chopped pecans (extra points if you toast them)	2	14	0	140
1/2 teaspoon ground cinnamon				
pinch ground cloves				
1/2 teaspoon vanilla extract				
1/4 teaspoon cream cheese flavor				
1/4 cup Swerve	0	0	48	0
Total	79	36	115	875
Half of that big old 24 oz Deluxe container	**39**	**18**	**58**	**438**

1. Measure all the base ingredients into your Creami container, making sure not to pass the max fill line.
2. Blend with your immersion (stick) blender til smooth and luscious.
3. Pop into your freezer for 24 hours.
4. Pop into your Ninja Creami Deluxe. Select full, make your selection, and hit the go button.
5. Take a peek. Perfectly creamy? Great! If not, add 1-2 Tablespoons of vanilla almond milk and select full and push the re-spin button. (Usually requires a re-spin.
6. Enjoy!

Tastes like pineapple cake, spice cake, and banana bread collided!

Makes a 24 oz Deluxe pint. Have a smaller 16 oz model? Cut all the ingredients to 2/3.

Dragon Fruit

	Protein	Fat	Carbs	Calories
1 cup 2% Daisy cottage cheese	26	5	10	180
2 scoops vanilla protein powder (Optimum Nutrition Whey)	48	3	8	240
2 cups frozen dragon fruit, thawed	2	1	32	136
2 T Swerve	0	0	24	0
Total	76	9	74	556
Half of that big old 24 oz Deluxe container	**38**	**5**	**37**	**278**

That color is totally natural! If you haven't tried dragon fruit before, It has a very mild earthy flavor.

1. Measure all the base ingredients into your Creami container, making sure not to pass the max fill line.
2. Blend with your immersion (stick) blender til smooth and luscious.
3. Pop into your freezer for 24 hours.
4. Pop into your Ninja Creami Deluxe. Select full, make your selection, and hit the go button.
5. Take a peek. Perfectly creamy? Great! If not, add 1-2 Tablespoons of vanilla almond milk and select full and push the re-spin button. (Usually requires a re-spin.
6. Enjoy!

Measure frozen fruit while it's frozen!!!

Makes a 24 oz Deluxe pint. Have a smaller 16 oz model? Cut all the ingredients to 2/3.

Passionfruit

	Protein	Fat	Carbs	Calories
1 cup 2% Daisy cottage cheese	26	5	10	180
2 scoops vanilla protein powder (Optimum Nutrition Whey)	48	3	8	240
2 cups frozen passionfruit, thawed	2	2	26	120
6 Tablespoons Swerve	0	0	72	0
Total	76	10	116	540
Half of that big old 24 oz Deluxe container	38	5	58	270

Passionfruit is an amazing combination of tropical and sour! I first had it as an exchange student in Australia and have missed it ever since. I was delighted when passionfruit pulp cubes showed up here in the freezer section! This is my favorite flavor!

1. Measure all the base ingredients into your Creami container, making sure not to pass the max fill line.
2. Blend with your immersion (stick) blender til smooth and luscious.
3. Pop into your freezer for 24 hours.
4. Pop into your Ninja Creami Deluxe. Select full, make your selection, and hit the go button.
5. Take a peek. Perfectly creamy? Great! If not, add 1-2 Tablespoons of vanilla almond milk and select full and push the re-spin button. (Usually requires a re-spin.
6. Enjoy!

Measure frozen fruit while it's frozen!!!

Makes a 24 oz Deluxe pint. Have a smaller 16 oz model? Cut all the ingredients to 2/3.

Coconut

Ingredient	Protein	Fat	Carbs	Calories
1 cup 2% Daisy cottage cheese	26	5	10	180
2 scoops vanilla protein powder (Optimum Nutrition Whey)	48	3	8	240
2 frozen coconut smoothie packets, thawed	2	14	12	180
1/2 cup vanilla almond milk	1	1	1	15
1/4 teaspoon Adams super strength coconut flavor				
1 Tablespoon Swerve	0	0	12	0
Total	77	23	43	615
Half of that big old 24 oz Deluxe container	38	12	21	308

1. Measure all the base ingredients into your Creami container, making sure not to pass the max fill line.
2. Blend with your immersion (stick) blender til smooth and luscious.
3. Pop into your freezer for 24 hours.
4. Pop into your Ninja Creami Deluxe. Select full, make your selection, and hit the go button.
5. Take a peek. Perfectly creamy? Great! If not, add 1-2 Tablespoons of vanilla almond milk and select full and push the re-spin button. (Usually requires a re-spin.
6. Enjoy!

Makes a 24 oz Deluxe pint. Have a smaller 16 oz model? Cut all the ingredients to 2/3.

Candied Orange Sweet Potato

Ingredient	Protein	Fat	Carbs	Calories
1 cup 2% Daisy cottage cheese	26	5	10	180
2 scoops marshmallow protein powder (Ryse Jet Puffed)	50	4	6	260
1 1/2 cups cooked mashed sweet potato	3	0	41	171
zest of 1/4 orange (OPTIONAL!)	0	0	1	2
1/4 cup orange juice (OPTIONAL!)	0	0	7	30
1/2 teaspoon ground cinnamon				
1/8 teaspoon ground nutmeg				
1/2 teaspoon butter extract				
1 teaspoon vanilla extract				
2 Tablespoons brown sugar Swerve	0	0	24	0
Total	80	9	88	643
Half of that big old 24 oz Deluxe container	40	5	44	321
Toppings: 2 Tablespoons chopped pecans	1	7	0	70
Toppings: 2 Max Mallows, chopped	1	0	5	15
Half with toppings	42	12	49	406

Toppings optional but fun!

1. Measure all the base ingredients (not toppings!) into your Creami container, making sure not to pass the max fill line.
2. Blend with your immersion (stick) blender til smooth and luscious.
3. Pop into your freezer for 24 hours.
4. Pop into your Ninja Creami Deluxe. Select full, make your selection, and hit the go button.
5. Take a peek. Perfectly creamy? Great! If not, add 1-2 Tablespoons of vanilla almond milk and select full and push the re-spin button. (Usually requires a re-spin.)
6. Enjoy!

I gave the best thing on the Thanksgiving table a good for you any day makeover!!!

Makes a 24 oz Deluxe pint. Have a smaller 16 oz model? Cut all the ingredients to 2/3.

Strawberry Special K

Ingredient	Protein	Fat	Carbs	Calories
1 cup 2% Daisy cottage cheese	26	5	10	180
2 scoops marshmallow protein powder (Ryse Jet Puffed)	50	4	6	260
1 1/2 cups frozen strawberries, thawed	0	0	18	68
1 cup Special K cereal	6	0	23	120
1 teaspoon strawberry extract				
2 Tablespoons Swerve	0	0	24	0
Total	82	9	81	628
Half of that big old 24 oz Deluxe container	41	5	41	314

More chopped up frozen strawberries make the cutest mix-in!

Measure frozen fruit while it's frozen!!!

1. Measure all the base ingredients (not mix-ins or toppings!) into your Creami container, making sure not to pass the max fill line.
2. Blend with your immersion (stick) blender til smooth and luscious.
3. Pop into your freezer for 24 hours.
4. Pop into your Ninja Creami Deluxe. Select full, make your selection, and hit the go button.
5. Take a peek. Perfectly creamy? Great! If not, add 1-2 Tablespoons of vanilla almond milk and select full and push the re-spin button. (Usually requires a re-spin.
6. Enjoy!

Makes a 24 oz Deluxe pint. Have a smaller 16 oz model? Cut all the ingredients to 2/3.

Special K

	Protein	Fat	Carbs	Calories
1 cup 2% Daisy cottage cheese	26	5	10	180
2 scoops marshmallow protein powder (Ryse Jet Puffed)	50	4	6	260
4 Tablespoons PB Fit	16	4	12	120
1 Tablespoon unsweetened cocoa powder	1	1	2	15
1 cup Special K cereal	6	0	23	120
2 Tablespoons Swerve	0	0	24	0
1 cup vanilla almond milk	1	3	1	30
Total	100	17	78	725
Half of that big old 24 oz Deluxe container	**50**	**8**	**39**	**363**

Optional toppings: more Special K, mini chocolate chips, butterscotch chips

1. Measure all the base ingredients into your Creami container, making sure not to pass the max fill line.
2. Blend with your immersion (stick) blender til smooth and luscious.
3. Pop into your freezer for 24 hours.
4. Pop into your Ninja Creami Deluxe. Select full, make your selection, and hit the go button.
5. Take a peek. Perfectly creamy? Great! If not, add 1-2 Tablespoons of vanilla almond milk and select full and push the re-spin button. (Usually requires a re-spin.
6. Enjoy!

Ice Cream for Breakfast Day is the first Saturday in February!

Makes a 24 oz Deluxe pint. Have a smaller 16 oz model? Cut all the ingredients to 2/3.

Mint Chocolate Chip

	Protein	Fat	Carbs	Calories
1 cup 2% Daisy cottage cheese	26	5	10	180
2 scoops vanilla protein powder (Optimum Nutrition Whey)	48	3	8	240
1 1/4 cups vanilla almond milk	1	3	1	38
1/2 teaspoon mint extract				
4 Tablespoons Swerve	0	0	48	0
Total	75	11	67	458
Half of that big old 24 oz Deluxe container	38	6	34	229
Mix-Ins! 2 Tablespoons mini chocolate chips per person	0	8	18	140
Half plus 2 Tablespoons mini chocolate chips per person	38	14	52	369

You can use sugar-free chocolate chips, but it only saves 20 calories, so….

1. Measure all the base ingredients (not mix-ins or toppings!) into your Creami container, making sure not to pass the max fill line.
2. Blend with your immersion (stick) blender til smooth and luscious.
3. Pop into your freezer for 24 hours.
4. Pop into your Ninja Creami Deluxe. Select full, make your selection, and hit the go button.
5. Take a peek. Perfectly creamy? Great! If not, add 1-2 Tablespoons of vanilla almond milk and select full and push the re-spin button. (Usually requires a re-spin.
6. Add in the **chopped up mix-ins** in a column up the center of the container and hit full, mix in.
7. Enjoy!

Green food coloring totally optional!

Makes a 24 oz Deluxe pint. Have a smaller 16 oz model? Cut all the ingredients to 2/3.

Lavender Honey

	Protein	Fat	Carbs	Calories
1 cup 2% Daisy cottage cheese	26	5	10	180
2 scoops vanilla protein powder (Optimum Nutrition Whey)	48	3	8	240
lavender honey *(recipe below ↓)*	0	0	104	383
1 cup vanilla almond milk	1	3	1	30
Total	75	11	123	833
Half of that big old 24 oz Deluxe container	**38**	**5**	**61**	**417**

lavender honey

6 Tablespoons honey

1/4 cup Anthony's French lavender

Heat honey in the microwave for 20-30 seconds til it starts to bubble (keep an eye on it!). Add lavender and let steep one hour. Microwave 20-30 seconds (keep an eye on it!). Strain, pressing the lavender to get all the honey out. Discard the lavender.

1. Measure all the base ingredients into your Creami container, making sure not to pass the max fill line.
2. Blend with your immersion (stick) blender til smooth and luscious.
3. Pop into your freezer for 24 hours.
4. Pop into your Ninja Creami Deluxe. Select full, make your selection, and hit the go button.
5. Take a peek. Perfectly creamy? Great! If not, add 1-2 Tablespoons of vanilla almond milk and select full and push the re-spin button. (Usually requires a re-spin.
6. Enjoy!

==Tiny bit of red and blue food coloring, totally optional!==

Makes a 24 oz Deluxe pint. Have a smaller 16 oz model? Cut all the ingredients to 2/3.

Chai

Ingredient	Protein	Fat	Carbs	Calories
1 cup 2% Daisy cottage cheese	26	5	10	180
2 scoops vanilla protein powder (Optimum Nutrition Whey)	48	3	8	240
1/4 cup sweetened condensed milk	6	6	44	260
1/2 teaspoon ground cardamom				
1/2 teaspoon ground ginger				
1/4 teaspoon ground cinnamon				
1/4 teaspoon ground cloves				
1 1/4 cup vanilla almond milk	1	3	1	38
Total	81	17	63	718
Half of that big old 24 oz Deluxe container	**41**	**9**	**32**	**359**

1. Measure all the base ingredients into your Creami container, making sure not to pass the max fill line.
2. Blend with your immersion (stick) blender til smooth and luscious.
3. Pop into your freezer for 24 hours.
4. Pop into your Ninja Creami Deluxe. Select full, make your selection, and hit the go button.
5. Take a peek. Perfectly creamy? Great! If not, add 1-2 Tablespoons of vanilla almond milk and select full and push the re-spin button. (Usually requires a re-spin.
6. Enjoy!

Makes a 24 oz Deluxe pint. Have a smaller 16 oz model? Cut all the ingredients to 2/3.

Coffee

	Protein	Fat	Carbs	Calories
1 cup 2% Daisy cottage cheese	26	5	10	180
2 scoops vanilla protein powder (Optimum Nutrition Whey)	48	3	8	240
1 cup strong brewed black coffee *(decaf is fine!!!)*	0	0	0	5
1/4 cup vanilla almond milk	0	1	0	8
1/4 cup Swerve	0	0	48	0
Total	74	9	66	433
Half of that big old 24 oz Deluxe container	37	4	33	216

You can add 2-4 Tablespoons of any syrup you love in your coffee instead of the swerve! We love sugar free Torani salted caramel, French vanilla, and brown sugar cinnamon!

1. Measure all the base ingredients into your Creami container, making sure not to pass the max fill line.
2. Blend with your immersion (stick) blender til smooth and luscious.
3. Pop into your freezer for 24 hours.
4. Pop into your Ninja Creami Deluxe. Select full, make your selection, and hit the go button.
5. Take a peek. Perfectly creamy? Great! If not, add 1-2 Tablespoons of vanilla almond milk and select full and push the re-spin button. (Usually requires a re-spin.
6. Enjoy!

Makes a 24 oz Deluxe pint. Have a smaller 16 oz model? Cut all the ingredients to 2/3.

Matcha

	Protein	Fat	Carbs	Calories
1 cup 2% Daisy cottage cheese	26	5	10	180
2 scoops vanilla protein powder (Optimum Nutrition Whey)	48	3	8	240
4 teaspoons matcha powder	0	0	8	34
1/4 cup Swerve	0	0	48	0
1 1/4 cups vanilla almond milk	1	3	1	38
Total	75	11	75	492
Half of that big old 24 oz Deluxe container	**38**	**6**	**38**	**246**

1. Measure all the base ingredients into your Creami container, making sure not to pass the max fill line.
2. Blend with your immersion (stick) blender til smooth and luscious.
3. Pop into your freezer for 24 hours.
4. Pop into your Ninja Creami Deluxe. Select full, make your selection, and hit the go button.
5. Take a peek. Perfectly creamy? Great! If not, add 1-2 Tablespoons of vanilla almond milk and select full and push the re-spin button. (Usually requires a re-spin.
6. Enjoy!

Makes a 24 oz Deluxe pint. Have a smaller 16 oz model? Cut all the ingredients to 2/3.

Butter Pecan

Ingredient	Protein	Fat	Carbs	Calories
1 cup 2% Daisy cottage cheese	26	5	10	180
2 scoops vanilla protein powder (Optimum Nutrition Whey)	48	3	8	240
1/2 cup toasted pecans	4	28	0	280
1 1/4 cups vanilla almond milk	1	3	1	38
3 Tablespoons brown sugar Swerve	0	0	36	0
1/2 teaspoon lorann super strength pecan flavor				
1 teaspoon butter extract				
Total	79	39	55	738
Half of that big old 24 oz Deluxe container	**40**	**20**	**28**	**369**

1. Measure all the base ingredients into your Creami container, making sure not to pass the max fill line.
2. Blend with your immersion (stick) blender til smooth and luscious.
3. Pop into your freezer for 24 hours.
4. Pop into your Ninja Creami Deluxe. Select full, make your selection, and hit the go button.
5. Take a peek. Perfectly creamy? Great! If not, add 1-2 Tablespoons of vanilla almond milk and select full and push the re-spin button. (Usually requires a re-spin.
6. Enjoy!

Pie crust pieces and whipped cream would make fun toppings if you're feeling extra!

Makes a 24 oz Deluxe pint. Have a smaller 16 oz model? Cut all the ingredients to 2/3.

Salted Caramel Pretzel

Ingredient	Protein	Fat	Carbs	Calories
1 cup 2% Daisy cottage cheese	26	5	10	180
2 scoops Salted Caramel protein powder (Quest)	52	1	6	240
2 Tablespoons sugar free salted caramel torani syrup	0	0	1	0
1 1/4 cups vanilla almond milk	1	3	1	38
Total	79	9	18	458
Half of that big old 24 oz Deluxe container	40	5	9	229
MIX-INS! 25 Ultra thin salty pretzel sticks per person	1	0	6	29
Topping! 1 squirt Jordan's skinny caramel sauce	0	0	0	0
Topping! 2 Max Mallow, burnt caramel flavor, chopped	1	0	5	15
Half plus mix-in and toppings	41	5	21	273

Jordan's Skinny Sauces makes a fun drizzle! It comes out of that bottle like an aggressive jet, so I increase the size of the hole.

1. Measure all the base ingredients (not mix-ins or toppings!) into your Creami container, making sure not to pass the max fill line.
2. Blend with your immersion (stick) blender til smooth and luscious.
3. Pop into your freezer for 24 hours.
4. Pop into your Ninja Creami Deluxe. Select full, make your selection, and hit the go button.
5. Take a peek. Perfectly creamy? Great! If not, add 1-2 Tablespoons of vanilla almond milk and select full and push the re-spin button. (Usually requires a re-spin.
6. Add in the **chopped up mix-ins** in a column up the center of the container and hit full, mix in.
7. Enjoy!

Makes a 24 oz Deluxe pint. Have a smaller 16 oz model? Cut all the ingredients to 2/3.

Gingerbread

Ingredient	Protein	Fat	Carbs	Calories
1 cup 2% Daisy cottage cheese	26	5	10	180
2 scoops vanilla protein powder (Optimum Nutrition Whey)	48	3	8	240
1 Tablespoon molasses	0	0	15	58
5 Tablespoons brown sugar swerve	0	0	60	0
1 teaspoon ground ginger				
1/4 teaspoon ground cinnamon				
pinch ground cloves				
1/2 teaspoon butter extract				
1 1/4 cups vanilla almond milk	1	3	1	38
Total	75	11	94	516
Half of that big old 24 oz Deluxe container	38	5	47	258
MIX-INS! 1/2 oz crystallized ginger per person	0	0	13	50
Half with mix-ins	38	5	60	308

1. Measure all the base ingredients (not mix-ins or toppings!) into your Creami container, making sure not to pass the max fill line.
2. Blend with your immersion (stick) blender til smooth and luscious.
3. Pop into your freezer for 24 hours.
4. Pop into your Ninja Creami Deluxe. Select full, make your selection, and hit the go button.
5. Take a peek. Perfectly creamy? Great! If not, add 1-2 Tablespoons of vanilla almond milk and select full and push the re-spin button. (Usually requires a re-spin.
6. Add in the **chopped up mix-ins** in a column up the center of the container and hit full, mix in.
7. Enjoy!

Makes a 24 oz Deluxe pint. Have a smaller 16 oz model? Cut all the ingredients to 2/3.

Chocolate Hazelnut

	Protein	Fat	Carbs	Calories
1 cup 2% Daisy cottage cheese	26	5	10	180
2 scoops chocolate protein powder (Optimum Nutrition whey)	48	4	6	240
1 Tablespoon unsweetened cocoa powder	1	1	2	15
1 cup chocolate almond milk	1	2	19	100
3 Tablespoons Swerve	0	0	36	0
1/2 cup hazelnuts	8	36	10	380
1 teaspoon vanilla				
Total	84	48	83	915
Half of that big old 24 oz Deluxe container	**42**	**24**	**42**	**458**

1. Measure all the base ingredients (not mix-ins or toppings!) into your Creami container, making sure not to pass the max fill line.
2. Blend with your immersion (stick) blender til smooth and luscious.
3. Pop into your freezer for 24 hours.
4. Pop into your Ninja Creami Deluxe. Select full, make your selection, and hit the go button.
5. Take a peek. Perfectly creamy? Great! If not, add 1-2 Tablespoons of vanilla almond milk and select full and push the re-spin button. (Usually requires a re-spin.
6. Enjoy!

Strawberries or bananas would make a fabulous topping!

Makes a 24 oz Deluxe pint. Have a smaller 16 oz model? Cut all the ingredients to 2/3.

Chocolate-Dipped Churro

	Protein	Fat	Carbs	Calories
1 cup 2% Daisy cottage cheese	26	5	10	180
2 scoops chocolate protein powder (Optimum Nutrition whey)	48	4	6	240
1 Tablespoon unsweetened cocoa powder	1	1	2	15
3 Tablespoons Swerve - brown sugar	0	0	36	0
3/4 teaspoon ground cinnamon				
1 1/2 teaspoons Lorann buttery sweet dough extract				
chocolate almond milk 1 1/4 c	1	3	24	125
Total	76	13	78	560
Half of that big old 24 oz Deluxe container	**38**	**7**	**39**	**280**

1. Measure all the base ingredients (not toppings!) into your Creami container, making sure not to pass the max fill line.
2. Blend with your immersion (stick) blender til smooth and luscious.
3. Pop into your freezer for 24 hours.
4. Pop into your Ninja Creami Deluxe. Select full, make your selection, and hit the go button.
5. Take a peek. Perfectly creamy? Great! If not, add 1-2 Tablespoons of vanilla almond milk and select full and push the re-spin button. (Usually requires a re-spin.
6. Add in the **chopped up churros (optional!)** in a column up the center of the container and hit full, mix in.
7. Enjoy!

These grain-free churro chips make a fun topping!

Makes a 24 oz Deluxe pint. Have a smaller 16 oz model? Cut all the ingredients to 2/3.

Loaded Chile Chocolate

Ingredient	Protein	Fat	Carbs	Calories
1 cup 2% Daisy cottage cheese	26	5	10	180
2 scoops chocolate protein powder (Optimum Nutrition whey)	48	4	6	240
1 Tablespoon unsweetened cocoa powder	1	1	2	15
3 Tablespoons Swerve - brown sugar	0	0	36	0
1/4 teaspoon ground chipotle				
1 1/4 cups chocolate almond milk	1	3	24	125
Total	76	13	78	560
Half of that big old 24 oz Deluxe container	38	7	39	280
MIX-INS! 25 Ultra thin salty pretzel sticks (about 1/6 c)/person	1	0	6	29
MIX-INS! 1 oz (about 1/4 cup) peanuts per person	7	14	5	160
Half with mix-ins	46	21	50	469

Don't like peanuts? Coconut plays really well in here, too!

1. Measure all the base ingredients (not mix-ins or toppings!) into your Creami container, making sure not to pass the max fill line.
2. Blend with your immersion (stick) blender til smooth and luscious.
3. Pop into your freezer for 24 hours.
4. Pop into your Ninja Creami Deluxe. Select full, make your selection, and hit the go button.
5. Take a peek. Perfectly creamy? Great! If not, add 1-2 Tablespoons of vanilla almond milk and select full and push the re-spin button. (Usually requires a re-spin.
6. Add in the **chopped up mix-ins** in a column up the center of the container and hit full, mix in.
7. Enjoy!

Makes a 24 oz Deluxe pint. Have a smaller 16 oz model? Cut all the ingredients to 2/3.

Kinda Feel Like an Almond Joy

Ingredient	Protein	Fat	Carbs	Calories
1 cup 2% Daisy cottage cheese	26	5	10	180
2 scoops chocolate protein powder (Optimum Nutrition whey)	48	4	6	240
1 Tablespoon unsweetened cocoa powder	1	1	2	15
3 Tablespoons Swerve	0	0	36	0
2 frozen coconut smoothie packets, thawed	2	14	12	180
1/2 teaspoon almond extract				
1/2 teaspoon Adams super strength coconut flavor				
3/4 cup chocolate almond milk	1	2	14	75
Total	78	26	80	690
Half of that big old 24 oz Deluxe container	**39**	**13**	**40**	**345**

1. Measure all the base ingredients (not mix-ins or toppings!) into your Creami container, making sure not to pass the max fill line.
2. Blend with your immersion (stick) blender til smooth and luscious.
3. Pop into your freezer for 24 hours.
4. Pop into your Ninja Creami Deluxe. Select full, make your selection, and hit the go button.
5. Take a peek. Perfectly creamy? Great! If not, add 1-2 Tablespoons of vanilla almond milk and select full and push the re-spin button. (Usually requires a re-spin.
6. Enjoy!

You kinda feel more like a Mounds? No problem! Just skip the almond extract. Done!

Makes a 24 oz Deluxe pint. Have a smaller 16 oz model? Cut all the ingredients to 2/3.

Okay. I've lived in Texas for a million years now, but I grew up in Wisconsin, and some of my childhood buddies really wanted a Wisconsin drink in protein ice cream form. I can't put a boozy concoction in a good-for-you book. Unless.... it's bonus content! So here it is, a bonus recipe...

A brandy slush is a holiday classic in Wisconsin. People mix up big batches of it in repurposed ice cream tubs, so it amuses me to turn it into a protein ice cream. Full circle, yeah? To serve it, you fill a glass with 1/2 slush (well, ice cream) and 1/2 7-Up.

Don't want alcohol? No problem! If there are kiddos in the house, people all over Wisconsin put the batch in two ice cream tubs, and only put brandy in one of them.

Jen's Protein Brandy Slush	Protein	Fat	Carbs	Calories
1 cup 2% Daisy cottage cheese	26	5	10	180
2 scoops vanilla protein powder (Optimum Nutrition Whey)	48	3	8	240
1 cup double strength tea *(2 teabags for 1 cup water)*	0	0	0	0
4 Tablespoons Swerve	0	0	48	0
1/4 cup orange juice concentrate	0	0	27	110
1/4 cup lemonade concentrate	0	0	20	80
1/4 cup brandy	0	0	0	128
Total	74	8	113	738
Half of that big old 24 oz Deluxe container	**37**	**4**	**57**	**369**
Same thing without the brandy.....				
Non-alcoholic Total	**74**	**8**	**113**	**610**
Half of that big old 24 oz Deluxe container	**37**	**4**	**57**	**305**

O&H Bakery in Racine, Wisconsin Supper Clubs Book (Supper clubs are the best! Order an Old Fashioned with your prime rib or fish!), Fish boil at White Gulf Inn in Fish Creek, Cave kayaking at Whitefish Dunes State Park, hydro bikes at Nicolet Beach, and Eagle Trail at Peninsula State Park. The last four are all Door County.

A few of my Wisconsin favorites…..

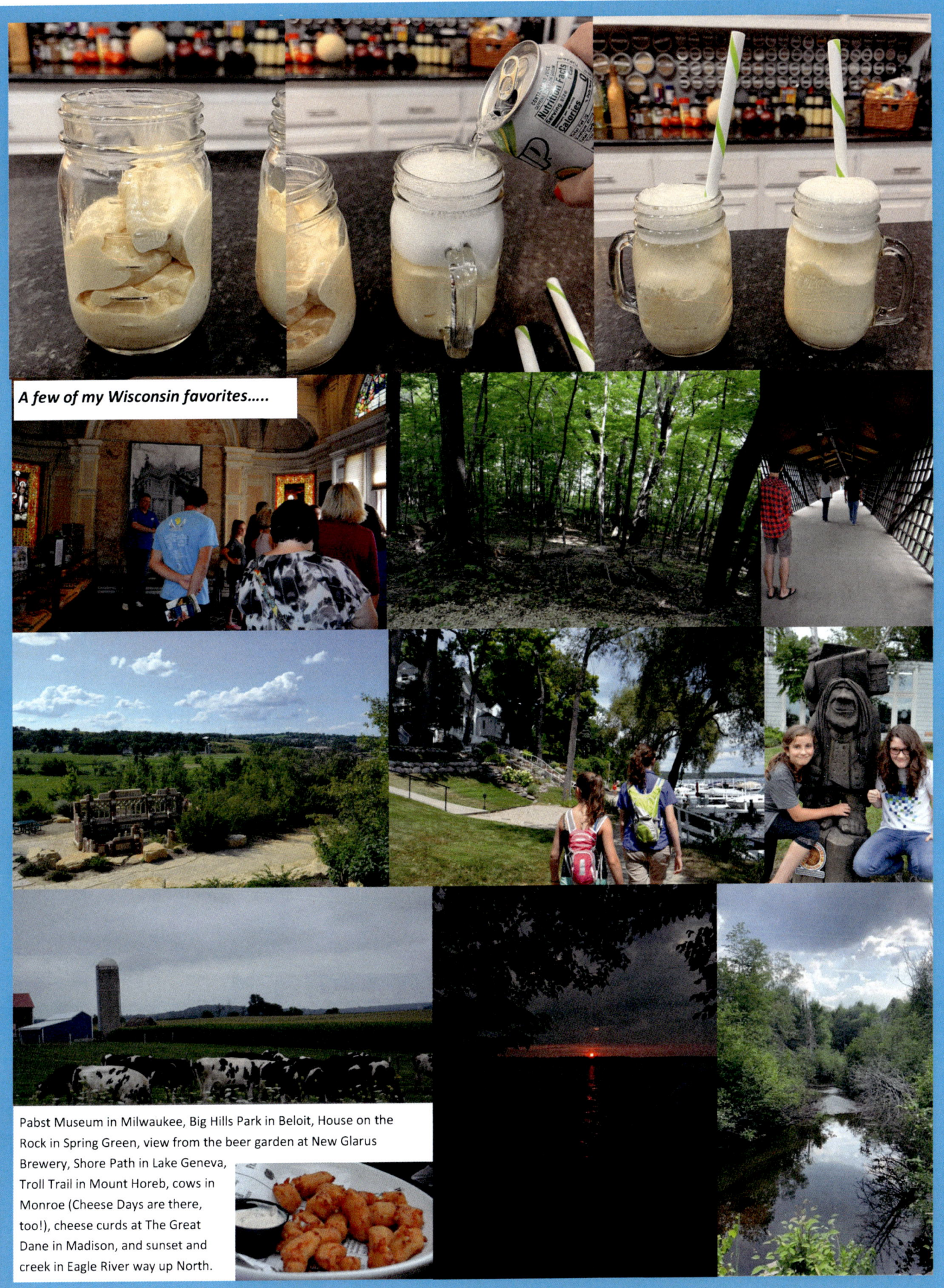

Pabst Museum in Milwaukee, Big Hills Park in Beloit, House on the Rock in Spring Green, view from the beer garden at New Glarus Brewery, Shore Path in Lake Geneva, Troll Trail in Mount Horeb, cows in Monroe (Cheese Days are there, too!), cheese curds at The Great Dane in Madison, and sunset and creek in Eagle River way up North.

41

Just leaving this little vegetable sculpture here that I did a few years back because he always gets people's attention. :D Thanks again for buying my book! I hope you love it! Please leave a review on Amazon if you're so inclined!

xx Jen

42

Jennifer Guerrero
the not so starving artist

Love this? Come find my blog! I'm a food blogger and cookbook reviewer! So many delicious recipes to try! No clickbait anywhere and no "jump to recipe" because there's no fluff. Just recipes with Amazon affiliate links for some of my kitchen favorites *after* the recipes.

The Not So Starving Artist

www.JenniferGuerrero.com

Instagram @starvingartisteats

Check out my other books!

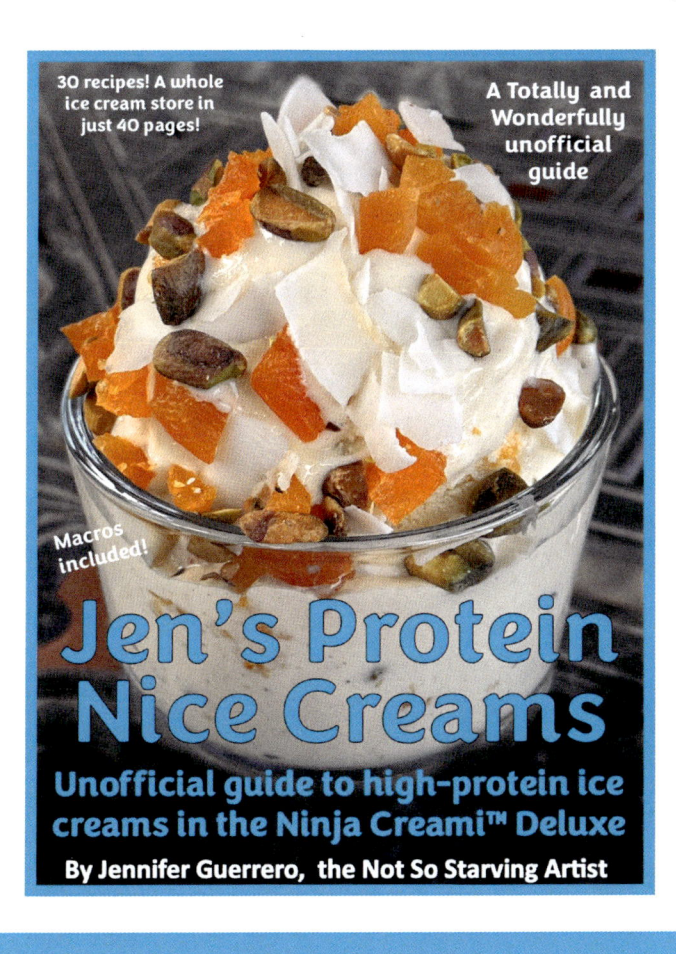

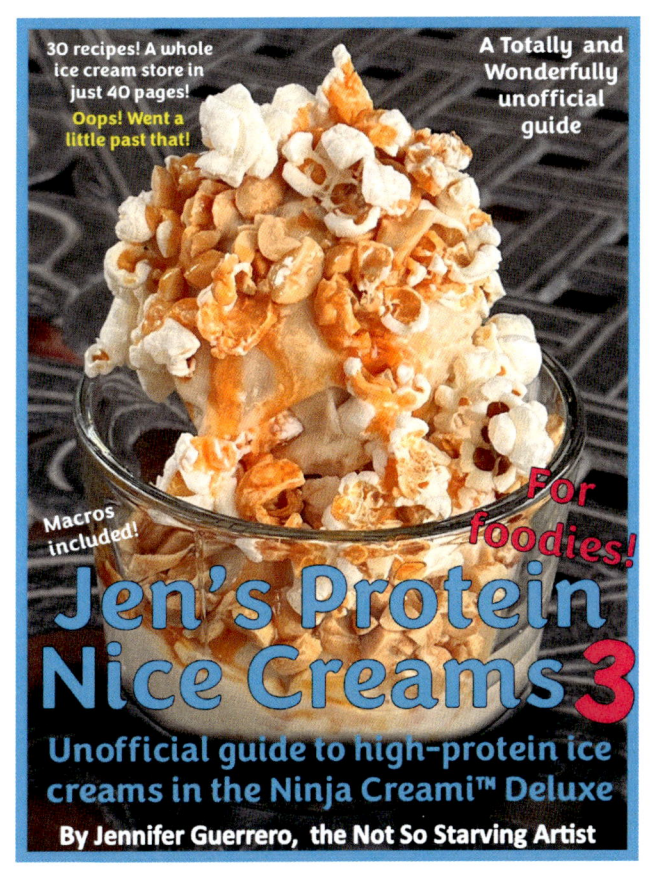

Made in the USA
Monee, IL
18 June 2025